D1065118

Off My Rocker and on My Knees

52 DEVOTIONS FOR DEVOTED GRANDMAS

BroadStreet
PUBLISHING

BroadStreet Publishing Group, LLC
Racine, Wisconsin, USA
BroadStreetPublishing.com

Off My Rocker—and on My Knees: 52 DEVOTIONS FOR DEVOTED GRANDMOTHERS

Copyright © 2017 BroadStreet Publishing Group

Written by Vicki Kuyper

ISBN-13: 978-1-4245-5320-4 (hardcover)
ISBN-13: 978-1-4245-5422-5 (e-book)

Stock or custom editions of BroadStreet Publishing titles may be purchased in bulk for educational, business, ministry, fundraising, or sales promotional use. For information, please e-mail info@broadstreetpublishing.com.

Cover design by Chris Garborg, garborgdesign.com
Interior design and typeset by Katherine Lloyd, theDESKonline.com

Printed in China
17 18 19 20 21 5 4 3 2 1

Contents

1

Off My Rocker— and on My Knees

Get down on your knees before the Master;
it's the only way you'll get on your feet.

—James 4:10 MSG

If grandmothers ran the world, our grandkids would always be within arm's reach—at least until we needed a little quiet time to relax and reenergize. But life doesn't often work out that way. Even if we live right around the corner, our grown children—and their children—lead busy lives. "Grandma Time" may never be as long, or frequent, as our hearts wish it would be. What's more, instead of living across town, grandkids often live across the country. Or even on the other side of the world.

In some instances, miles don't separate us from the little ones we love. It's fractured family relationships. Perhaps the time between visits is measured in years. Perhaps they've stopped altogether.

Regardless of what separates us, God provides a wonderful way to hold our grandchildren close, even when we're far apart: prayer. To begin, all we need to do is get on our knees before God's throne. We don't have to literally get down onto the floor, especially if we'd have to pray for the strength to get back up again! But we do need to humble our hearts, figuratively kneeling before the almighty God who loves our grandchildren even more than we do. That means we can trust him with all of their tomorrows, as well as whatever is on our heart concerning them today.

Prayer is more than asking God to keep our grandkids happy and healthy. It's a way of strengthening a three-way relationship between God, our grandkids, and ourselves. As we talk to our heavenly Father about the grandkids he's graciously brought into our lives, he transforms our worries and longings while transforming us. Through prayer, God helps us mature into the grandmothers our grandchildren need us to be.

Dear Lord, thank you for the family you've given me, each and every one, big and small. Help me place every concern I have about them into your able hands today. Amen.

LOVE IN ACTION

Set a specific time to pray for your grandchildren each day. Let them know when that time is. Then, whenever they notice that time on the clock, they'll think of you thinking of them—which draws you all closer to each other and to God.

2

Let a Little Child Lead You

"Take off your shoes,
for you are standing on holy ground."

—Exodus 3:5 TLB

Grandchildren are an invitation to worship. Their curiosity and wonder help reveal the holiness God has hidden all around us: The wildflower tenaciously growing through a hairline crack in the pavement. The bee that dances on fragile flower petals then nimbly takes flight, carrying with it half of its body weight in pollen. A grandchild's delighted giggle when toddling barefoot across the lawn for the very first time.

Children help remind us that there's nothing ordinary

about an "ordinary day." We're constantly surrounded by miracles, a gallery of masterworks created by an almighty Artist. As we grow older, it's easy to become accustomed to the world we live in, to mistake what's familiar with the commonplace. But through God's gift of grandchildren, we can humbly become students and allow our grandkids to lead us and teach us. Through their eyes and experiences, we can relearn to see the world around us—and God's hand at work in it—in fresh and wonderful ways.

Vincent van Gogh said: "If one feels the need of something grand, something infinite, something that makes one feel aware of God, one need not go far to find it. I think sometimes I see something deeper, more infinite, more eternal than the ocean in the expression of the eyes of a little baby when it wakes in the morning, and coos or laughs because it sees the sun shining on its cradle."[*]

From the moment of birth, each grandchild has so much to teach us, so many unexplored journeys to take us on. Let's kick off our shoes, grab their tiny hands, and allow them to lead us back to the wonder of worship, closer to the heart of an infinitely creative, innovative God.

---

[*] Vincent van Gogh, quoted in Debora Silverman, *Van Gogh and Gauguin: The Search for Sacred Art* (New York: Farrar, Straus and Giroux, 2000), 173.

Dear Lord, help me pay attention to the lessons you want to teach me through my grandchildren. Reawaken my heart and soul to a deeper level of worship and awe. Amen.

LOVE IN ACTION

Play hide-and-seek with your grandkids in a whole new way. Take a walk in the park or around the block and search for little unexpected treasures hidden along the way. Together, thank God for each one.

3

Spoiler Alert!

Every good and perfect gift is from above, coming
down from the Father of the heavenly lights, who
does not change like shifting shadows.

—JAMES 1:17

We've all seen the T-shirts. Perhaps there's one hiding
in your very own closet. The words may differ, but
the message is the same: "Nana's the Name and Spoiling
Is My Game!" It seems to be a grandparent's rite of passage to extend to our kids' kids everything we withheld
from our own children when they were young. Candy
before dinnertime. That overpriced, made-to-break "toy
of the moment." Ten bucks to blow on anything they
want. We bend the rules and empty our pocketbooks, all
in the name of love.

But is love really what's driving us? Or are we simply using our grandkids as an excuse to shop? Maybe it's our own desire to be loved pushing us to try to buy our way into the "favorite grandparent" slot. Or perhaps we honestly believe that accumulating stuff and getting our own way is what will make us, and our grandkids, happy.

How we show love to our grandkids may be how we expect God to show his love for us. Yes, God blesses us beyond measure. But that doesn't mean he fulfills our every wish and whim, treating our prayers like a Christmas gift wish list. He loves us so much that he wants what's best for us, what will help our hearts become more like his. Sometimes that means providing things that give us great joy. Other times that means allowing difficult, painful situations to enter and continue in our lives, coaxing us to grow and mature. Often our greatest challenges can give birth to our greatest strengths.

Let's love our grandchildren the way God loves us—unconditionally, sacrificially, and wisely. And let's remember how much our heavenly Father loves us, in good times as well as bad.

Dear Lord, teach me to love my grandkids from the purest, truest part of myself—the part of my heart that most resembles you. Teach me that at times, the word *no* can be an act of love too. Amen.

LOVE IN ACTION

The next time you're tempted to buy your grandkids something, ask God to show you the whys behind your potential purchase. If those reasons fall short of what you believe pleases God, ask him to show you another way to lavish your grandkids with love—and act on that.

4

Return to Sender

"I prayed for this child, and the LORD
has granted me what I asked of him."

—1 SAMUEL 1:27

In the book of 1 Samuel, we're told that Hannah, one of Elkanah's two wives, was barren. For years Elkanah's other wife, Peninnah, provoked Hannah, trying to make her feel inferior and often bringing Hannah to tears. Hannah brought her tears and heartfelt longings to God in prayer, and as Hannah's words in verse 27 attest, God answered her prayers with a son. She named him Samuel, which in Hebrew sounds similar to the phrase "heard by God."

But verse 27 doesn't tell the whole story. Hannah continues in verse 28, "So now I give him to the Lord. For his whole life he will be given over to the Lord." After Samuel was weaned, Hannah brought her living, breathing answer to prayer back to the temple. There she handed him over to Eli the priest, who would raise Samuel to adulthood as a servant of the Lord. Out of gratitude for God's gift, she gave that gift right back to him.

Like Hannah, we've prayed for a child—a grandchild. And God has graciously granted our request. We can't help but have dreams for those grandchildren ... that they'd be healthy and happy, have families of their own, succeed in their endeavors, and follow in the footsteps of their heavenly Father. But our dreams may not always line up with God's will or the free will of our grandchildren. That's just one reason to adopt Hannah's prayer as our own.

By dedicating our grandchildren to God, we recognize that these precious children are not really ours. They are not even wholly their parents'. First and foremost, they're God's. They are his unique creation, dearly loved and fully known. By giving them "back" to God, we're simply acknowledging his sovereignty in their lives—and ours.

Dear Lord, for these grandchildren I prayed—and will continue to pray. I release them into your hands, to love and to lead. Amen.

LOVE IN ACTION

Repeat Hannah's prayer from 1 Samuel 1:27-28 for each one of your grandchildren. You may want to commit these verses to memory and repeat them to yourself each time you need to be reminded of who really holds your grandchildren's hopes and dreams in his hands.

5

Story Time

Our children and their children will get in on this
as the word is passed along from parent to child.
Babies not yet conceived will hear the good news—
that God does what he says.

—Psalm 22:30–31 msg

"Grandma, tell me a story!" When we hear those magic words, we have so many options. We can grab a book off the shelf, snuggle up close, and begin to read. We can make up our very own fairy tale, one where our grandchild pursues adventure and winds up the hero. Or we can tell a true story, one we've lived firsthand—one that illustrates a time in our life when God has proven himself to be our very own Hero. After all, history is made of *history*, including our own.

To tell a story that engages others, we first need to be engaged by it ourselves. What's your faith story? When did you first encounter God? Why do you believe he's real? When have you seen God working in a unique way in your own life? If your walk of faith was a kid's story-book, what would your favorite adventures be?

Jesus knew the power of story to help others connect with God. Matthew 13:10–13 tells us:

> The disciples came up and asked: "Why do you tell stories?" [Jesus] replied, "You've been given insight into God's kingdom. You know how it works. Not everybody has this gift, this insight; it hasn't been given to them. Whenever someone has a ready heart for this, the insights and understandings flow freely. But if there is no readiness, any trace of receptivity soon disappears. That's why I tell stories: to create readiness, to nudge the people toward receptive insight." (MSG)

Give your grandkids a nudge toward better under-standing their heavenly Father. Help them see that he lives outside the pages of the Bible and flannel board at church, that he lives in you—and he can live in them too.

Dear Lord, help me be more aware of how you've been a part of my story throughout my life. Then, please help me share that story with others, including my grandkids. Amen.

LOVE IN ACTION

Write out episodes of your personal faith story in a way that will capture a child's heart and imagination. If you're feeling crafty, add photos or artwork (perhaps your grandchildren's) and have it printed up online through a photo-book site. That way your grandchildren can hear or read the tale when you're not by their side.

6

Photo Finish

Do not be interested only in your own life,
but be interested in the lives of others.

—Philippians 2:4 icb

Every grandmother knows that *her* grandkids are the cutest, smartest, and most exceptional children ever born. And today, Grandma no longer has to wait for the mailman to deliver that highly anticipated envelope stuffed with the latest photos of her pride and joy. Now she has a cell phone filled with more adorable images than any purse-sized brag book could ever hope to hold.

Lucky us! Through the power of social media, we can now share those images with the whole world. Multiple times a day. We can post our grandkids' pictures and videos on Facebook, use their faces to adorn our cell phone screens, and have their sweet images replicated on anything from purses to puzzles, T-shirts to tea towels. Why settle for idealizing our grandkids when we can idolize them?

Okay, when you put it that way, we all know that's a line we don't care to cross. But when does affection cross over into obsession? Especially with grandkids? After all, it's a grandma's job, and privilege, to gush a little. We've waited a long time for this pleasure. But when our pleasure incites others to roll their eyes, we've become takers instead of givers, self-centered instead of other centered. If we're honest, being excessively focused on our grandkids can be a roundabout way of focusing on ourselves. After all, they are *our* grandkids. How cute, smart, and extraordinary they are reflects positively on us.

If our life is all about the grandkids, however, our life is too small. God has created us to love family, friends, and strangers—as well as him. Each morning, pray for God's love to flow through you to whomever he brings your way.

Dear Lord, help my love for my grandkids truly be about them, not me. And help me love them, and others, in ways that bring glory to you. Amen.

LOVE IN ACTION

Learn to communicate with your grandkids in the way they're most comfortable communicating. Feel free to send cards through the mail, but also master using Skype, social media, and texting. Just remember, everything in moderation!

7

Mimsy: Pro Wrestler

He determines the number of the stars
and calls them each by name.

—PSALM 147:4

"Grandma" used to be the generally accepted title for women with grandchildren. Now Granny's branched out. Whether we're known as Nana, Mimi, G'Ma, or Mimsy, our moniker is dear to us. It's more than a name. It's a title that signifies a loving role we play in a little one's life. Sure, we still bear our original given name of Pamela, Karen, or Sue, but our new name describes a new side of us in terms of a new relationship.

From what we read in the Bible, it appears God

appreciates this kind of new relationship/new name change as well. Consider when Abram becomes Abraham. Sarai becomes Sarah. Simon becomes Peter. These name changes matter because they signify a change in character and purpose. Take Jacob. After a very close encounter with God, his name was changed to Israel, which means "struggles or wrestles with God." What will our name come to mean in the life of a child?

One thing we can do to make our name become dear to the child who says it, is to follow in Israel's footsteps—by daring to wrestle with God. To wrestle, we have to engage with someone, be close enough to touch them, consider what they're doing, and discover how their actions affect our own.

Wrestling doesn't have to be contentious. This isn't a match with a winner and a loser. Wrestling with God means asking questions, refusing to become stagnant in our faith, and measuring what we hear against God's Word as we measure our own lives the same way. It means we're willing to admit when we're wrong and ready to change when God asks. Regardless of what she's called, that describes a grandmother whose name is synonymous with "victory."

Dear Lord, make me a grandmother who's worthy of bearing your name as a Christian. When my grandkids think of me, may they automatically also think of you. Amen.

LOVE IN ACTION

Choose a special nickname for each of your grand-children. Although names like Chunky Monkey and Pouty Princess can easily slip into use, carefully select a positive one, a name that your grandchild will long to live up to.

8

It's All a Phase

There is a right time for everything.
Everything on earth has its special season.
There is a time to be born
and a time to die.

—Ecclesiastes 3:1–2 ICB

Every season of life has its struggles and its joys. A new-born grandbaby is sweet to cuddle, but she can try your patience with her tears in the middle of the night. An adventurous toddler can bring out the child in you, right before he breaks your favorite vase. Teenage grandchildren can surprise you with unexpected laughter, as well as bewildering bouts of anger. In trying to console our grown children with the fact that difficult seasons of parenthood are "only a phase," we may find that we're encouraging them (and ourselves) to focus on the future instead of the moment we're experiencing right now.

We know firsthand how fast time flies. Not so long ago, we rocked our own children to sleep instead of our grandchildren. But in what feels like the blink of an eye, we somehow became the older generation. So, let's do our best to help the younger generation slow down and savor this moment with their own children—even if the moment is a tough one.

Be honest about how difficult parenting can be. Remind your own children of phases they went through as they grew—and what you did as a parent to help them mature. Share your mistakes, as well as your hard-won victories. Apologize if you need to. Help them strategize if they want your help. Pray for God's perspective for everyone involved. Then, take a deep breath and live.

Whatever phase your grandkids, your kids, or you are in right now, it's where you are. There's no getting around it. You can only go through it, so accept it. Then, slow down long enough to look for the unique treasures God's hidden in the midst of your current chaos. They may never come again.

Dear Lord, every moment is a gift from You. Help me open each one I receive with joy, courage, curiosity, and gratitude. Amen.

LOVE IN ACTION

Don't be a fair-weather grandma. When your grandkids are going through a difficult stage, ask their parents what you can do to help. Keep drawing closer to your grandkids in creative ways, even if they're going through a phase where they're tempted to push you away.

9

Priceless Inheritance

A good life gets passed
on to the grandchildren.

—Proverbs 13:22 msg

An antique bureau. A strand of great-grandma's pearls.
The family cabin on the lake. A trust fund for college
tuition. When we talk about leaving our grandchildren
an inheritance, we're usually referring to some asset of
financial or sentimental value that we plan to pass on to
the next generation, presumably after we've discovered
what heaven is really like firsthand. When we "pass on,"
it only makes sense to pass down what's left behind. No
casket ever towed a moving van.

But what about the inheritance we're passing on
today? Every minute we spend with our grandkids (or

anyone else, for that matter) we leave something behind. We leave a memory. Whether that memory serves as a positive example or a cautionary tale is up to us. Yes, it's great to give and serve and pray and talk about God with our grandkids. However, doing it for the purpose of being seen is not the point.

Jesus said:

When you pray, do not be like those who only pretend to be holy. They love to stand and pray in the synagogues and on the street corners. They want to be seen by other people. What I'm about to tell you is true. They have received their complete reward. (Matthew 6:5 NIRV)

Our reward, and the one worth passing down, comes from being authentic, a real-life work in progress that's being transformed each day through God's power and love. Our words, our actions, our attitudes—they reveal who we truly are. If they don't line up with who we wish we were, there's still time. Remember, if we're still alive, God's not done yet!

The only footsteps worth following in are those that lead closer to God. Let's leave our grandchildren a clear path that leads straight to God's loving arms.

Dear Lord, it's easy for me to confuse what I do with who I am. Please work on me from the inside out, making me more like you. Amen.

LOVE IN ACTION

Spend some time today considering what kind of spiritual inheritance you hope to pass on to your grandchildren. Then ask God to help you become the woman he created you to be, day by day.

Food for Thought

Feed the hungry! Help those in trouble! Then your
light will shine out from the darkness, and the
darkness around you shall be as bright as day.

—Isaiah 58:10 TLB

Our grandkids are blessed. After all, they have us as
grandmas! We'll go above and beyond to meet their
needs—and often, their wants. Though financial situations differ from one grandparent to the next, chances
are, if you're reading this book, you have at least some
disposable income. But there are plenty of other "grand"
kids around the world whose grandparents, and parents,
are unable to provide even the basic necessities for their
family, necessities many of us take for granted each day.

According to the United Nations, about twenty-one thousand people die of hunger or hunger-related causes every day—about four people every second—and the majority of them are children. Add the effects of war and poverty, sexual or physical abuse, inadequate medical care and education, and the challenges many children face around the globe are enough to break a grandmother's heart. And they should. They certainly break God's.

Throughout the Bible, God calls for his children to care for widows and orphans, to provide for the poor, and to feed the hungry. He asks us to be his hands and feet to those in need, whether they live right next door or somewhere we've only heard about in the news. While it's true we can't single-handedly save the world, we can make a positive difference in it. And we can help inspire our grandchildren to do the same.

Instead of focusing solely on making certain our own grandkids are well taken care of, let's expand our definition of family. Let's find at least one way to regularly share a grandmother's love, and God's, with children in need. Let's not put it off any longer. Every second matters.

Dear Lord, help me to not be so overwhelmed by the extent of the problem that I sit back and do nothing. Show me how to share my love, and resources, in a way that truly makes a positive difference in your world. Amen.

LOVE IN ACTION

Help your grandkids better understand the needs of children around the world by sponsoring a child through a relief organization, such as Compassion International. Request a child whose age is close to your grandchild's and then regularly write letters together. You can pray for your sponsored child together too.

When Your Worst Dreams Come True

If your heart is broken, you'll find GOD right there;
if you're kicked in the gut, he'll help you catch your breath.

—PSALM 34:18 MSG

Being a grandmother means expanding our definition of love in a whole new way. It means cherishing every breath, every step, and every stage of some very precious little lives. But life is filled with the unexpected. Sometimes sorrow and heartache catch us by surprise. The deeper our love, the deeper our grief when someone we love is hurting or—dare we even think it?—heads home to heaven before we do.

There are many verses in the Bible that assure us of

God's protection and healing. So when bad things happen to those we love, including our grandchildren, we often find ourselves caught off guard. We're confused. Hurt. Angry. Lost. We shake our fist, or at least our head, at God. We question the validity of prayer. But tragedy isn't God's final word. Eternity is. It's God's perpetual protection and ultimate healing that lead us safely home to him.

That doesn't mean God takes our current grief and suffering lightly. Jesus himself is described as "a man of sorrows, acquainted with deepest grief" (Isaiah 53:3 NLT). This Man of Sorrows tells us:

> Everything I've taught you is so that the peace which is in me will be in you and will give you great confidence as you rest in me. For in this unbelieving world you will experience trouble and sorrows, but you must be courageous, for I have conquered the world! (John 16:33 TPT)

If we risk loving others, including our grandchildren, our heart will break somewhere along the way. When that happens, Jesus encourages us to rest in him. Even if we don't have the energy, or words, to pray, we can lean on God and his promises. Only God can create a seemingly impossible peace from the pieces of a broken heart.

Dear Lord, I pray for your protection for my grandchildren, in every area of their lives. But when I experience firsthand how broken this world is, show me how to rest amid chaos, to reside in your peace, regardless of my circumstances. Amen.

LOVE IN ACTION

When your grandchild's heart is broken, whether over something as small as losing a toy or as big as their parents' divorce, be an oasis of Jesus' peace and rest for them. Don't feel as though you have to fix everything to make it better. Simply hold them, pray with them, listen to them, and assure them of your (and God's) never-ending love.

12

The Language of Love

Jesus felt sorry for the man. So he touched him
and said, "I want to heal you. Be healed!"

—Mark 1:41 icb

God created kids to be cuddled. Why else would he have
designed babies so cute and snuggly? To feed them, we
have to hold them close. To ease their crying, we rock
them in our arms. Even before babies can understand
what we're saying, we communicate with them through
touch. It's a language we need to engage in throughout
our lives—and a language Jesus used in unexpectedly
powerful ways.

When Jesus walked on this earth, contracting leprosy
meant being ostracized and isolated. The disease was considered incurable and a curse from God. Lepers could not

come within six feet of uninfected people, including their own families. That distance expanded to 150 feet if the wind was blowing! Lepers were required to live outside of the community and weren't allowed to speak to other people, except to shout, "Unclean!" This warned others that those with leprosy were nearby. After all, to touch a leper would make you unclean, which meant you were unfit and unacceptable to be in God's presence. At least, that's what everyone believed.

But Jesus knew the truth. He knew God's love and acceptance extended to everyone, including those considered "untouchable." So even though Jesus could have healed the leper with a word, he reached out and touched a man thought to be unclean. While Jesus' divine power healed the man of his disease, his touch must have gone a long way in healing the man's heavy heart.

As grandmothers, may we learn to reach out physically to others in a way that helps and heals. May we overcome our own reservations and inhibitions to be able to encourage, comfort, and celebrate others without saying a word.

Dear Lord, thank you for giving me an example of what "loving well" means, as recorded in the Gospels. Teach me how to better communicate through the gift of tender, loving touch. Amen.

LOVE IN ACTION

As our grandkids get older, they may feel more uncomfortable or embarrassed about cuddling with Grandma. So, come up with a special "I love you" touch that's acceptable. Perhaps it's a thumb squeeze or a high five. Whatever it is, make a loving touch part of every interaction you have with them.

13

Forget Decorum ... Let's Play!

One day some parents brought their children to Jesus
so he could touch and bless them. But the disciples
scolded the parents for bothering him. When Jesus
saw what was happening, he was angry with his disciples. He said to them, "Let the children come to me.
Don't stop them! For the Kingdom of God belongs to
those who are like these children."

—MARK 10:13–14 NLT

In New Testament times, it was traditional for young children to be brought to the local rabbi to be blessed. So why
were the disciples so bent out of shape when parents brought
their children to Jesus for this very reason? Undoubtedly,
the disciples felt there were better uses for Jesus' time. But
Jesus' own words in the Gospel of Mark tell a different story.

Jesus reminds us that children are not distractions, interruptions, or impositions. They're worth God's time—and ours. Not only that, these sweet little carefree beings, who are totally dependent on others to care for their needs, are examples of what faith is all about. They believe what we say, trust in our love, and are honest about how they feel. They also embrace life wholeheartedly, without inhibitions. If they're in the mood to dance down the street, they don't worry about what people will think. They don't let a bad hair day or a hand-me-down swimsuit get in the way of celebrating the gift of today.

As we age, it's easy to forget the joy and importance of play. Grandkids can help us remember, if we let them. So let's dare to get down on the floor, even if we need help getting back up. Let's wear the silly hat, drink imaginary tea, and fight invisible monsters with nothing but pipe cleaners and soda straws. Let's paint with our fingers and wade barefoot in streams, giggle, grin, tell stories, and dream. Let's wriggle into that swimsuit and forget about our cellulite. And if the grandkids ask what those funny lines are on our thighs, let's tell them they're a map leading to hidden treasure! Let's enjoy life—and let our grandchildren lead the way.

Dear Lord, you are the author of creativity and joy. Please help me care less about how old I am or what others may think and more about celebrating the gift of life and love you've so graciously given. Amen.

LOVE IN ACTION

Become the playmate your grandkids want to hang out with. Jot down ideas for games, crafts, and adventurous outings on three-by-five index cards and keep them in a folder. When it's time for a visit, keep a couple of ideas on hand to use as time allows.

14

A Word of Advice

Trust in the LORD with all your heart;
do not depend on your own understanding.
Seek his will in all you do,
and he will show you which path to take.

—PROVERBS 3:5–6 NLT

Our kids may be grown with children of their own, but we've still been around the block a time or two more than they have. At the very least! That's why advice comes so easily to a grandmother's lips. We really do know more than our kids do. Okay, so maybe not about gaming, Snapchat, and how to reprogram our phone, but about important stuff, like parenting. So, it makes perfect sense that we should bless our children with the benefit of our knowledge and experience, right?

It depends. Advice can be a welcome gift or a divisive wedge, depending on our timing, methods, and motives. So before we open our mouths, let's check our hearts. Should we speak or remain silent? If we're quiet and patient enough to allow God's Spirit to speak, we may discover that our own understanding of the situation doesn't tell the whole story.

Young parents, especially those who've only recently had their first child, are already feeling rather overwhelmed, emotional, and sleep deprived. They're also trying to put into practice everything they've read, heard, and experienced so far. Perhaps we can best support them by asking questions—and being humble enough to learn from their response. After all, times have changed since we were parents. These days, our grandchild is likely to be delivered by a midwife instead of a doctor. Baby wearing, co-sleeping, and baby massage are "in."

Instead of swooping in to advise our children on the "correct" way to comfort, feed, discipline, or nurture their own children, we should sit back and learn a thing or two. We can freely share our own experiences and opinions—when we're asked for them.

Dear Lord, show me how to continue to nurture my own children wisely now that they're grown. Teach me how to support and encourage them by knowing when to speak and when to hold my tongue. Amen.

LOVE IN ACTION

One way of giving advice in a nonjudgmental manner is to give your children a baby book when they have kids of their own. Include tips, techniques, and parenting stories from when they were young. That way, they're free to follow your advice—or simply chuckle over it in the privacy of their own home.

15

Nana Diva

Run from temptations that capture young people.
Always do the right thing. Be faithful, loving,
and easy to get along with.

—2 Timothy 2:22 cev

We're familiar with the stereotype: young parents dreading a visit from a demanding mother or mother-in-law. For you, it may be more than a stereotype. It may be a chapter from your very own story. But whether we've lived it firsthand or chuckled over an awkward encounter depicted on TV, let's refuse to play the lead in this family drama. Let's ditch the diva within and step willingly into a servant's shoes.

It's true that grandmothers can be creaky servants. We're slower than we used to be. We consider multitasking doing anything else in addition to breathing. We may not be able to get down on our knees to scrub the floor or pick up itty-bitty interlocking blocks, but that doesn't mean we resign ourselves to the easy chair and expect the world to revolve around us.

As we get older, and maybe spend much of our time alone, we may crave being the center of attention, being pampered, and being waited on hand and foot. But that reality marks the life of a newborn, not a Christ-centered older woman. As the years pass, let's truly grow wiser and become less of a diva, not more.

One way we can do that is by regarding our visits with the grandkids as working vacations. Yes, let's anticipate laughing and playing together, but let's also offer to change a diaper, rock a fussy child so Mom can nap, or babysit so Mom and Dad can spend a night out. Let's continue extending grace and not throw a fit over incidentals, like not receiving a hand-written thank-you note from the grandkids for every gift we give. Then, when we say our good-byes, our kids won't thank God that we're leaving, but that he made us family.

Dear Lord, even though I may need more help as I age, show me how I can continue to help and serve others. Continue to shape my me-centered heart into more of a Christ-centered one. Amen.

LOVE IN ACTION

Instead of always bringing gifts for the grandkids, bring along something to help their parents. For instance, prepare a meal that can be frozen and easily reheated to serve on a busy evening.

16

Playing Favorites

My brothers and sisters, practice your faith
in our glorious Lord Jesus Christ by not favoring
one person over another.

—JAMES 2:1 GW

We know we shouldn't play favorites, but let's be honest: it's the foundation for most of our relationships. We choose whom to include in our circle of friends because we "favor" those people over others who've crossed our path. We'd be wise to do the same when choosing our spouse! To a certain degree, we even play favorites when it comes to choosing a doctor, hair stylist, real estate agent, or church home.

Family is different. If we favor one child—or grandchild—over another, feelings get hurt. Competitions erupt. Relationships, and self-esteem, suffer. While it may be perfectly natural to feel a stronger affinity for some people more than others, giving one person preferential treatment over another is where God says stop.

We may feel pangs of partiality toward the only grand-daughter in a passel of grandsons, the bookish grandchild over the rambunctious one, or our biological grandchild over a step-grandchild we haven't had the opportunity to meet until later in life. Feelings are neither right nor wrong. It's what we do with them that matters.

The English word *emotion* comes from the Latin root word *exmovēre*, which means "to move out, move away."* Where will we allow our emotions to lead us? What will they inspire us to do and say? Let's ask God to use them to challenge us to work harder toward developing a deeper connection with those we find it more difficult to love. Love is never wasted. We may find that those we had to work hardest to love become those closest to our heart.

---

* *Webster's Third New International Dictionary, Unabridged*, "emotion," http://unabridged.merriam-webster.com.

Dear Lord, help me to love each one of my grandchildren as the amazingly unique creation you designed them to be. Teach me how to show them individually how lovable they are, in your eyes and mine. Amen.

LOVE IN ACTION

Recognize that your grandkids have the same temptation to "play favorites" that you do. You may not be their favorite grandparent! Instead of allowing yourself to compete for first place, relax and simply be the person God created you to be—and encourage your grandchildren to do the same.

17

Gift Wrapped in Love

Watch the way you talk. Let nothing foul or dirty
come out of your mouth.
Say only what helps, each word a gift.

—Ephesians 4:29 MSG

Picture this: It's Christmas morning, and your grandkids are excited about opening the gifts you've placed under the tree. Imagine their expressions when your teenage grandson opens a trash bag filled with lawn clippings, your five-year-old granddaughter unwraps a case of wine, and their newborn sibling is presented with a set of carving knives. Totally inappropriate, right?

Sometimes our words are as well. If each word we speak is a gift, shouldn't we be thoughtful enough to choose those that fit just right before handing them out?

Words have power. They can hurt or heal, hinder or help. Which ones will we choose to bestow, especially on those we love?

Foul language isn't only made up of four-letter words. It can include negative attitudes, hateful prejudices, thoughtless gossip, or subtle put-downs. Or perhaps our witty sarcasm is getting lost in translation, or our constructive criticism is actually tearing down those around us instead of building them up. We may not mean to give inappropriate gifts like these to our grandchildren, but they can slip right off our tongue without us even noticing.

Instead of spell-check, we need a heart-check. We need to ask God to help us hear ourselves the way others do. One way we can do that is to ask a close friend, one who truly knows how to "tell it in love" (Ephesians 4:15 MSG), to speak truthfully to us. Do we have any blind spots when it comes to our tongue? How about our tone or our timing when speaking to others?

Let's allow God to help slow us down and think before we speak. Sometimes we may find that slowing down prevents us from saying anything at all—and that in itself may be the perfect gift.

Dear Lord, I know how easily words slip right through my lips. Help me slow down and think before I speak, so each word I say, even the tough ones, will be a welcome gift. Amen.

LOVE IN ACTION

We want to relax and be ourselves with our grandkids, but let's bring the best of ourselves into their presence. Memorize James 1:19: "Everyone should be quick to listen, slow to speak and slow to become angry." Repeat this verse silently to yourself each time you come into contact with your grandchildren.

18

For Mature Audiences Only

"I will be your God through all your lifetime,
yes, even when your hair is white with age.
I made you and I will care for you.
I will carry you along and be your Savior."

—Isaiah 46:4 TLB

When we were kids, grandmothers seemed ancient. At least in our minds. We thought our parents were old—and our grandparents were even older than that! They had gray hair, flabby arms, and wrinkly hands. Some could even remove their teeth to make us laugh. But now that we're the grandparents in question, old age doesn't seem quite so funny. It also doesn't feel as though it applies to us. "Old" always seems to be somewhere further down the road than our birth certificates say we are right now.

It's true that as grandmothers today, we're likely to be more active and in better physical shape than our parents were at our age. But that doesn't mean we haven't begun to feel the passage of time. Aging happens. If we're blessed, it happens to us. Every year is a gift, even if it gets a bit harder as the decades roll by. Do we view each new age with appreciation and anticipation? Or do we believe that the "good old days" are all behind us?

The way we view growing older has an effect on the quality of our lives—and those of our grandkids. It teaches them what older people are like, as well as what their own future may hold. Like every stage our grandkids go through, there will be joys and challenges during this stage of maturity for us. Yet God remains as close, and as faithful, as ever. We may even find that the new challenges we face during this season cause us to lean on God more heavily than ever before. This isn't a sign of weakness but of strength. It demonstrates to our grandkids the sanctity of life, from beginning to end, and the tender devotion of our steadfast God.

Dear Lord, you know the challenges I face as the years go by. Help me lean on you each day and continue to discover fresh, new reasons for thanks and praise. Amen.

LOVE IN ACTION

Play a game with your grandkids where you ask them to act like you, while you act like them. Watch closely what they do and say. See if there are any negative characteristics they act out that you may need to address. Meanwhile, have a great time acting like a kid! Don't let your inhibitions hold you back.

19

Hero Worship

The LORD your God is with you.
He is a hero who saves you.
He happily rejoices over you,
renews you with his love,
and celebrates over you with shouts of joy.

—ZEPHANIAH 3:17 GW

Thanks to the influence of comic books and movies, most of today's kids go through a superhero phase. It's one way for young minds to grapple with adult-sized issues, such as: Am I safe? How can I tell the good guys from the bad guys? Is there a power greater than my mom and dad? Is there a hero hiding inside of me?

As mature women devoted to God, we recognize these questions can't be answered by someone wearing a cape and tights, but by the one and only almighty God. He's the only true Superhero. What's more, with his power at work in our lives, God can bring out the hero in each of us—including our grandchildren.

Every child of God, young or old, is both a good guy and a bad guy. We can serve God or ourselves, be generous or selfish, encourage or criticize. We can be a hero and a villain, sometimes all in the same day. When we blow it, whether through an honest mistake or a bad choice, that's when it's important to take off our mask. It's time to own up to what we've said or done, apologize, and make things right—even if it means humbling ourselves in front of our grandkids.

True heroes aren't puffed up with false pride; rather, they are aware of the flaws in their own character. While it's true that as some people get older, they become more stuck in their ways, may this never be true of us. May we continue to grow, becoming examples of humility, teachability, courage, and grace under pressure. As we do, our grandkids will better understand that faith is the only true superpower available to them in this life.

Dear Lord, please bring out the hero in me. Help me learn how to humbly depend on you, lean into your strength, and risk doing the right thing, regardless of the cost. Amen.

LOVE IN ACTION

The next time a new superhero movie comes out, talk to your grandkids about the ways the specific crime fighter is like, or different from, Jesus. Then, discuss how God can bring out the everyday hero in each one of them.

20

Make a Joyful Noise

So go ahead everyone and shout
out your praises with joy!

Break out of the box and let loose
with the most joyous sound of praise!

Sing your melody of praise to the Lord,
and make music like never before!

—Psalm 98:4–6 TPT

It's been said that music is the universal language, but it's far grander than that. Music transcends the physical world and soars straight into the spiritual world, where it inexplicably touches God's own heart. Throughout the Bible, we can tell that music is not just handy for dancing. It's also designed for worship. Perhaps that's one of the reasons God so fondly described David, the author of the biblical songbook of Psalms, as "a man after [his] own heart" (Acts 13:22).

Music moves God—and it moves us. Whether we're a tone-deaf toddler, a teen with a hand-me-down electric guitar, or a grandmother who still has a cassette deck in her car, music has power. It can move us to dance, dream, clap, cry, or sing along. It can move us to praise God with psalms of our own.

Even in secular music, there's an echo of something sacred that has the ability to connect us with its original Creator. We can help our grandchildren tap into that connection by helping them better understand the power behind the music they listen to. But first, we have to become acquainted with that music ourselves.

Ask your grandkids to introduce you to the kinds of music they like best (even if it's out of your musical comfort zone). Ask what they like about it and how it makes them feel. Then, talk about how they think God feels about the music and the message. Don't get judgy. Instead, really listen. Ask yourself the same questions about your own musical selections.

Let's allow the soundtrack of our grandchildren's lives, and ours, to become a talking point that challenges all of us to recognize God's power and presence in the details.

Dear Lord, thank you for your gift of music. Help me and my grandkids to use it wisely in our lives. Amen.

LOVE IN ACTION

Be daring—download some of your grandchildren's favorite songs onto your own playlist. Listen until you can sing along, so you can carry on an informed discussion with them about how what we put in our minds and hearts draws us closer to, or further away, from God.

21

Faith in Action

We must show love through actions that are sincere,
not through empty words.

—1 JOHN 3:18 GW

If we're grandmothers who are devoted to God, as well as our grandchildren, our desire will be for each of our grandkids to know Christ in a personal way. But not all parents will share that desire. Some are struggling with their own rocky road of faith. They may have wandered away from God, pushed him away, or can't quite grasp the reality of an almighty, eternal Creator.

If our grown children are opposed to us sharing our faith openly with their children, we need to honor their wishes—and allow our actions to preach where our words cannot. This doesn't mean we make certain we're "caught" reading the Bible or that we make a show of praying before meals. If we're acting pious to make a point, our actions are not sincere. Instead, let's ask for God's unconditional love to shine through us. That means accepting those we love where they are, right here, right now. We may not approve of everything they're doing, but our love shouldn't be based on their actions. It's not what determines their worth in our eyes or God's.

Our hearts may feel heavy because we believe it's our responsibility to lead the whole family to faith in God. That's an honorable intention. But it isn't a burden we're intended to carry. There's only one Holy Spirit—and it isn't us! Paul wrote in 1 Corinthians 3:6, "My work was to plant the seed in your hearts, and Apollos' work was to water it, but it was God, not we, who made the garden grow in your hearts" (TLB). We have a role to play in sharing our faith with those we love. But their choice, and their growth, is out of our hands.

Dear Lord, I want those I love to know the joy of loving you. Please use me in whatever way is appropriate and effective to point them in your direction. Amen.

LOVE IN ACTION

Whether or not our child or grandchild is a prodigal, faithful prayer and unconditional love should always be at the heart of our relationship. Set aside time each week to pray specifically for the individual spiritual journeys of those we love, and for the wisdom we need to know how to "show" instead of "tell" others about God.

22

Our Pride and Joy

Grandchildren are the crown of grandparents,
and parents are the glory of their children.

—Proverbs 17:6 GW

Grandchildren are like priceless jewels set in a glorious crown of joy. Wearing the crown of grandparenthood can inspire us to stand a little taller, a little prouder. But what's the true source of that pride?

It's easy to boast about how attractive our grandchildren are, how well they sleep through the night, the awards they've received at school, or how accomplished they are at sports or dance or marching band. But our grandchildren are more than what they do. The most precious thing about them is who they are.

When we focus solely on their accomplishments, we do them a disservice. We may encourage a sense of competition and comparison among them. They may come to believe that being "above average" in every area of their lives is expected, instead of wholly improbable. They may also become hesitant to share their struggles or failures with us, fearing our pride in them will be diminished if we know the truth—that they're just like every other kid: human.

Our grandchildren are incredibly flawless jewels in our eyes, not because they're perfect but because of our deep love for them. That love makes us want to know, and celebrate, everything about them. So let's remember to applaud their character, as well as their GPA. When they're kind, honest, generous, or thoughtful, when they work very hard at something and don't succeed, when their unique qualities shine in an unconventional way, let's make certain they know how brightly they shine in our eyes—and God's.

Dear Lord, thank you so much for these amazing grandchildren you've brought into my life. Help me celebrate them, and encourage them, in ways that will make you proud. Amen.

LOVE IN ACTION

Make a special certificate, medal, trophy, or crown that honors something unique about each grandchild. Make sure to award something that might easily go unrecognized, but that is worthy of a grandmother's praise.

23

Three Little Words

No one can explain how a baby breathes before it is
born. So how can anyone explain what God does?
After all, he created everything.

—ECCLESIASTES 11:5 CEV

There are three little words every grandmother needs to
use without hesitation. Yes, "I love you" is important.
But so is, "I don't know." Regardless of how intelligent,
educated, well traveled, or experienced we are (or think
we are!), there will always be questions we cannot answer.
This is particularly true when it comes to God.

Faith and fact are not at opposite ends of what we
know to be true. They intersect over and over again. But
not everything we believe about God can be proven in a
way that meets the scientific standards we rely on today.

Of course, at one time people wholeheartedly believed the world was flat, the sun revolved around the earth, and that smoking was a healthy form of relaxation. Chances are pretty good that by the time our grandchildren are grown, many things we believe today will also prove to be false.

Regardless of how much is discovered in generations to come, God and his ways will always remain beyond scientific proof because they're beyond our comprehension. The Creator of the universe is simply too big for our brains to hold. But that can't stop our hearts and souls from responding to the mystery, and majesty, of his presence in this world. It can't stop us from asking, is there more to life than we can see with our eyes?

Let's not shy away from getting into spiritual conversations with our grandkids that may end with the words "I don't know." Instead, let's set them in motion. Let's learn what we can from God's Word, share what we've experienced on our spiritual journey, and get comfortable with unanswered questions. It's the only way we'll discover what part "wonder" plays in a wonderful life.

Dear Lord, teach me how to trust and believe what I can't prove or see. Also, help me to be honest enough, and humble enough, to say the words "I don't know." Amen.

LOVE IN ACTION

With your grandkids, come up with a list of questions you'd like to ask God. Then, search for answers together in Scripture. For the questions you cannot find answers to, pray. Ask God for understanding or for the peace we need to live with unanswered questions.

24

Special Delivery

Like a cool drink of water when you're worn out and
weary is a letter from a long-lost friend.

—Proverbs 25:25 msg

When it comes to spending time with someone we
love, including our grandkids, in person is always
best. But it's not always possible. That doesn't mean our
relationship can't continue growing closer even when
we're miles apart. All it takes is a little time and effort,
and a few pointers from the apostle Paul.

Paul was a master communicator. In the book of Acts,
we witness his impressive speaking ability in front of a
crowd. But when Paul was out of town, he stayed in touch
with those he cared about. Paul wrote letters of instruc-
tion, admonishment, and encouragement to the churches

in Ephesus, Corinth, and Rome, to name but a few. He also wrote to friends, including Timothy, Titus, and Philemon. But these weren't the only people who benefitted from Paul putting his God-inspired thoughts into writing. Today, we're still reading Paul's letters, memorizing them, being challenged by them, and applying the spiritual principles he shared to our own lives.

Keeping in contact with our grandkids through e-mail, text, and video chat is wonderful, but sending a card or letter to them through trusty old snail mail gives them something they can hold onto and read again and again. It's a touchstone, a physical reminder of how much they're loved.

Jokes, stickers, Bible verses, a comic strip, a fallen leaf, a silly original poem … there are so many things besides our best wishes that we can send their way. Even if our grandchild is too young to open an envelope by himself, we can begin writing letters, sending along our thoughts and prayers for this precious little person to enjoy one day. Let's join forces with our local mail carrier and deliver a little bit of love today!

Dear Lord, please inspire me with creative ways to connect with my grandkids in between visits. Help our relationship grow stronger with every passing year. Amen.

LOVE IN ACTION

Try to send a card or letter to your grandkids every month. Once this becomes a habit, you'll find yourself collecting little odds and ends through-out the month to send along with your thoughts and prayers.

25

A Commotion
of Emotion

With tender humility and quiet patience,
always demonstrate gentleness and generous love
toward one another, especially toward those
who may try your patience.

—EPHESIANS 4:2 TPT

Kids' emotions can ebb and flow like the ocean. They can be giggling one minute and inconsolable the next. We don't have to ask how they're feeling. We can see it on their faces, in the way they eat their lunch, and in the cadence of their walk.

Since our grandchildren's emotional state can seem as changeable as the weather in the Rockies, it's easy to minimize what they're going through. After all, a dripping ice cream cone doesn't signal the end of the world, and puppy love probably won't last until adulthood. We're tempted to pat them on the shoulder, explain that things really aren't as bad as they seem, and try distracting them with whatever amusement we find close at hand.

But when it comes to emotions, nothing seems small—if it's happening to us. That's why we need to do our best to empathize, instead of minimize, what our grandkids are going through. Sure, there will be stages of childhood where our grandkids will be rocked by temper tantrums, sobbing because they're overtired, or disrespectfully snarky because hormones go on an adolescent rampage. While it's important to be aware of what's going on behind the scenes physically and mentally, it's just as important to remember what it's like to walk a mile in their little shoes.

Empathy begins with pulling our grandkids in close, looking them in the eye, and asking them to tell us all about what's going on in their lives. Sometimes just being able to talk freely about how we feel, while nestled safely in the arms of someone we love, can help calm an emotional storm. Let's empathize instead of patronize. We never want to look down on our grandkids, regardless of how small they are.

Dear Lord, you know my grandkids inside and out. When they're struggling emotionally, please provide me with patience and insight, and guide me in how to best extend your comfort and compassion. Amen.

LOVE IN ACTION

Read articles online or from a childhood development book regarding the current age and stage of each of your grandchildren. Being better acquainted with what's "normal" for kids their age will help you treat them with greater wisdom, compassion, and understanding.

26

Just Say Whoa!

The news about Jesus spread even more.
Large crowds gathered to hear him and have their
diseases cured. But he would go away to places
where he could be alone for prayer.

—Luke 5:15–16 GW

A grandmother's love is a well that runs deep. Where our grandkids are involved, we want to fix every problem, fulfill every wish, dry every tear, and always answer yes. But that's not always possible—or even best. Though we long for our grandchildren to be happy, healthy, and to love us as much as we love them, true love sets limits.

Just look at God. His love for us runs deeper than ours ever could. Unlike us, he even has the ability to make every dream come true; but he doesn't give all of his children grand homes, fancy cars, and heartbreak-free lives. Though Scripture tells us that "where the Spirit of the Lord is, there is freedom" (2 Cor. 3:17 ICB), God also says there are things we shouldn't do, such as lie, steal, or envy what those around us happen to own. He sets limits on himself and us. He loves us enough to say no.

God also set limits for himself when he walked this earth as a man. Though Jesus cared deeply about those suffering around him, he also had to care for his human body. He took time to sleep, to pray, to eat, and to converse with his friends.

What limits do we need to set? Our grandkids may plead with us to purchase the latest and greatest new toy. Our grown children may ask us to cosign a loan or babysit while they're on vacation. We may have the ability, and even the desire, to say yes. But before we do, let's consider if it's the best way to show love for them, ourselves, and God.

Dear Lord, I know that love sometimes needs to say no. Please give me the wisdom to know when it's appropriate, and the courage to follow through—even if those I love may be pressuring me to answer yes. Amen.

LOVE IN ACTION

Get in the habit of just saying Whoa! to yourself when your kids or grandkids ask for something you're unsure you should give. Tell them you will pray about it before giving them an answer—then do.

27

Listen and Learn

Older women must train the younger women
to love their husbands and their children.

—TITUS 2:4 NLT

As older women, it's wonderful to be able to mentor the younger women in our lives. But regardless of how old we are, there's always someone older still! That means it's never too late to be a younger woman in an older woman's life.

When we were young mothers, women with older children showed us the ropes. Now that we're grandmothers, there are great-grandmothers who can do the same. They have so much to teach us. If only we'd ask …

There are many amazing woman who are sitting quietly on the sidelines. Once their bodies slow down, they begin to feel out of touch with the mainstream of life. The more isolated they become, the less they feel they've left to give. But these women are wellsprings of experience. God can use them mightily in our lives—and us in theirs.

To tap into their wisdom, we first need to welcome their friendship. That means intentionally reaching out. Think of the godly older women on the outer edges of your life. Is there someone God brings to mind who's in your church, around your neighborhood, or perhaps in your circle of friends? Arrange a time to get together. Ask about her life. Let her regale you with stories of her past. Listen and learn. If God so leads, ask if she'd consider being a mentor to you, someone who would help you become the grandmother you want to be. Then, ask if there's anything you can do for her. What does she need at this season in her life?

Friendship, and even mentorship, is a give-and-take relationship. Whether we're one or one hundred, we all have something to teach and something to learn.

Dear Lord, your Word tells us that "without counsel, plans go awry, but in the multitude of counselors they are established" (Prov. 15:22 NKJV). Please help build a circle of godly women of all ages into my life. Amen.

LOVE IN ACTION

Ask God to bring an older woman to mind who could be a positive, godly influence in your life. Then see how receptive she is to the idea. Don't just think of a mentor as someone who pours into your life. Resolve to be a blessing in her life as well.

28

Tomorrow's Unwritten

For we are God's masterpiece. He has created us
anew in Christ Jesus, so we can do the good
things he planned for us long ago.

—EPHESIANS 2:10 NLT

Having a grandchild can make us fall in love with the
human race all over again. When we look into those
little eyes for the very first time, we see the future. Our
heart swells with the promise of unlimited potential.
Who knows who this little person will grow up to be?

Our very own grandchild could discover the cure for
cancer, explore the outer regions of our solar system, feed
the hungry in a distant land, write a symphony that will
be played in concert halls for generations to come, or
become a parent to someone who does something equally

as wonderful. The scenarios we write in our minds are only limited by our imagination. But with God, the limits for their lives are boundless.

So much potential in such an adorable little package! Then why is it so easy to view grown-ups in a lesser light? Once children hit adulthood, we often view them as "what you see is what you get." The tattooed server at the pizza parlor, the homeless man in the park, the inmate serving time ... each one of these people was once a new-born, someone with promise and potential. The truth is, they still are.

As long as we live, each one of us holds the potential for growth and change. We still have the capability to make a positive difference in this world, whether heralded by the masses or quietly in the background. Let's not discount the potential, or worth, of any individual because of what we see with our eyes. Let's view everyone we meet with the eyes of a grandmother—someone who sees beyond today to the possibilities of tomorrow. Someone who knows that with God, anything is possible.

Dear Lord, help me see your best in others, including your very own image. Then, please show me how to help others better see that beauty and potential in themselves. Amen.

LOVE IN ACTION

Turn people watching into a positive pastime with your grandkids by playing "Here's What I See!" Challenge each grandkid to come up with a possible future for people that walk by—a future filled with God's very best.

29

A Little Bit of Heaven

"There are many rooms in my Father's house.
I wouldn't tell you this, unless it was true.
I am going there to prepare a place for each of you."

—JOHN 14:2 CEV

Jesus finished the Passover meal with his disciples. He'd explained how he was soon going to die. Understandably, his friends were confused and upset, so Jesus offered them comfort by giving them a hint as to what he had in store for them. He explained how they'd be together again one day, and that he was preparing a special place for each of them: their very own home in heaven.

We aren't ready for heaven quite yet, but that doesn't mean we can't do our best to give our grandkids a little piece of it here and now. We can prepare a special place for each of them, one where they can find comfort, know they're loved, and feel welcomed and at home. Whether we live in a mansion, a condo, or a double-wide doesn't matter. What's important is the love inside.

We can make a trip to Grandma's more memorable by preparing a "special spot" for our grandkids. It could be a guest room decorated with their artwork or simply a favorite treat placed on their pillow. If our home is small, we could place a child-sized beanbag chair in a cozy corner, set a picnic by the fireplace, make a tent out of blankets, or simply place a basket on the kitchen table filled with books, puzzles, DVDs, and games chosen especially for them.

When someone prepares a place for us, it means our arrival is anticipated. It shows we're on someone's mind even before we're in their presence. Whether it's Jesus or us making the preparations, it's just one more way of showing how much we care.

Dear Lord, help me know how to make my grandkids feel welcome, happy, and at home when they visit. Give me the energy, creativity, and patience I need to make our visits a joy for all of us. Amen.

LOVE IN ACTION

Consider what "a little bit of heaven" would feel like to each of your grandkids. Prepare a special spot for each of them, somewhere they'll anticipate spending time during their visit. There's no need to spend a lot of money—just some time, creativity, and love.

30

Who's in Charge?

Children, obey your parents;
this is the right thing to do because God
has placed them in authority over you.

—Ephesians 6:1 tlb

Even the best-behaved grandchild needs discipline at times, but being a grandma puts us in a tricky spot. After all, parents are the ones God put in charge of raising and disciplining their own children. Not us. However, when our grandkids start to "act up," we may automatically fall back on what we did back when our kids were young. For better or for worse.

Times have changed since we raised our own kids—or since we were kids ourselves. Back in the day, "spare the rod and spoil the child" was used as a biblical mandate to support spanking as a form of discipline. Though this phrase is based on Proverbs 13:24, the Contemporary English Version paraphrases this verse as, "If you love your children, you will correct them; if you don't love them, you won't correct them." That's the heart of God's intent: loving correction, not corporeal punishment.

We need to support our grown children in their efforts to lovingly guide our grandkids toward maturity. That means having a discussion with them about how they want us to discipline their children when they're not around. We need to respect their authority, just as their own children should.

We also need to carefully differentiate between accidents, immaturity, and direct disobedience. Mistakes happen, kids test limits, and good kids can do bad things. That doesn't make them bad kids, just kids in need of loving correction.

God knows the same is true of us. We're grandmothers, not kids, and we still don't always do what we know our heavenly Father would like us to. We need to keep that in mind when our grandkids push their parents' boundaries, and ours. We all can use a little loving correction now and then.

Dear Lord, thank you for loving me enough to correct me when I'm headed the wrong way. Please teach me how to do the same for my grandkids. Amen.

LOVE IN ACTION

After disciplining your grandkids, always take a moment after emotions have calmed down and any time-outs have ended to reaffirm your love for them—and remind them that you, their parents, and God know they're better than the poor decision they just made.

31

Heavenly Hotline

"This is your Father you are dealing with,
and he knows better than you what you need.
With a God like this loving you,
you can pray very simply. Like this:
Our Father in heaven, reveal who you are."

—MATTHEW 6:8–9 MSG

Grandkids can be a catalyst to prayer. Even grand-mothers who don't profess to believe in God can find themselves crying out to heaven for help if those they love are in trouble or in pain. God designed us that way. It's as if he imprinted his home phone number on speed dial in every human heart. When life is more than we can handle on our own, we automatically dial that number—even if we're unsure of who's on the other end.

When we commit to following Christ, we know whom we're calling, so we no longer reserve those calls just for emergencies. We pray for our grandchildren, even when life is going well. But instead of just praying *for* them, it's important for us to pray *with* them. It's one way we can help make them more comfortable calling on God on their own.

Jesus helped his disciples understand the necessity and simplicity of talking to our heavenly Father when he shared what we call the Lord's Prayer (Matthew 6:9–13; Luke 11:1–13). Jesus' example demonstrates that prayer doesn't require us to fold our hands or get on our knees. We don't need lofty words or lengthy petitions. All we need to do is thank God for who he is and what he's done, and ask him for what we need, including his forgiveness.

Instead of reserving prayer for mealtimes and calamities, let's talk to God freely and frequently in the presence of our grandkids. Even a simple "thank you for the gift of today" can be a lesson in loving communication for your grandkids, as well as a welcome gift to God.

Dear Lord, thank you for allowing us to come into your presence and communicate with you so easily. Help me take the time to stop and talk to you throughout the day, and please help my grandkids become comfortable doing the same. Amen.

LOVE IN ACTION

Regularly ask your grandchildren for prayer requests—any concerns they'd like you to take to God in prayer before you meet again. Then, share with them one thing you would like them to pray about for you. The next time you're together, be sure to ask for an update on what you've been praying about.

Burdens and Blessings

When others are happy, be happy with them.
If they are sad, share their sorrow.

—Romans 12:15 TLB

Being a grandmother, especially right after the birth of a new grandchild, can be a giddy experience. We gush, we boast, we brag ... we drone on and on to whomever will listen about what an incomparable blessing we've just received. But not everyone will share in the joy of our good news.

There are so many wonderful women around the world who would make amazing mothers and grandmothers but never receive the opportunity. Circumstances like infertility, the death of a child, divorce, or singleness can place a mantle of grief over the topic of grandparenting.

For them, yet another birth announcement, baby photo on Facebook, or grandmother's glad tidings feels like an indictment of failure or a calling card for heartbreak.

It's true that Romans 12:15 encourages us to "rejoice with those who rejoice." But it's far easier for those who are happy to comfort those who mourn. Those who are grieving may find it difficult to muster up the energy and sincerity needed to celebrate with those whose lives are currently bursting with joy. This is especially true when it comes to news that may reopen some very deep wounds.

Let's not allow ourselves to get so caught up in the bliss of our own situation that we're blind to the struggles of those around us. Instead, may the joy we feel serve as a constant reminder of how very blessed we are—and may its overflow inspire us to become an even richer source of encouragement and comfort for those who need it most.

Dear Lord, please show me how to use the joy you've brought into my life to do more than simply make me feel good. Use it to help me celebrate with others who are joyful and comfort those whose hearts are heavy. Amen.

LOVE IN ACTION

Keep a stack of sympathy, encouragement, and "thinking of you" greeting cards on hand. When you notice a friend or a grandchild fighting a difficult emotional battle, follow up any conversations you have by sending a card. Let them know they're in your thoughts and prayers.

33

The Source of Joy

Just one day of intimacy with you
is like a thousand days of joy rolled into one!
—PSALM 84:10 TPT

Think of your grandkids. Yup, right now. Chances are, a little smile is tugging at the corner of your mouth and a flutter of joy is doing the cha-cha in your heart. Perhaps a tear is even threatening to roll down your cheek because you wish you could be in their presence this very minute. Grandkids will do that to you.

But does thinking about God do that to us? Do we find as much joy in our relationship with God as we do with our grandkids? Do we smile just thinking about him? Do we long to spend time with him? Or are we like spoiled grandchildren who only call when we want something?

Building a relationship with someone we can't see, hear, or touch can be tough. Though God is always right beside us, it can be easy to forget he's even there. He isn't pushy. He waits for us to come to him. When we do, when we take the time to read his Word and bare our hearts in prayer, we're reminded of how much we need him—and long for him. The more consistent we are in spending time with God, the more easily we'll recognize his voice guiding us, see his hand at work in our lives, and feel his presence with us throughout the day.

Grandchildren are an incredible blessing, but our Savior, Creator, and almighty Father is the only everlasting source of joy in this world. Everything we treasure, everything we are, and everything we hope to be begins and ends in him. As we draw closer to our grandchildren, let's endeavor to remember to draw closer to the one who brought the gift of grandparenting into our lives.

Dear Lord, I want to look forward to spending time with you, and not regard my quiet time as just another obligation on my to-do list. Forgive me for my inattention and teach me how to love you deeply and sincerely. Amen.

LOVE IN ACTION

Loving God well helps us love everyone better, including our grandchildren. If you haven't already, set a time and place to draw near to God each day through prayer and studying his Word.

34

Healthy Habits

So whether you eat or drink or whatever you do,
do it all for the glory of God.

—1 CORINTHIANS 10:31

Grandmothers seem to be inextricably linked to baked goods. Particularly cookies. Maybe it's just a stereotype, but all grandmothers have an inkling as to how this stereotype got started. We like to treat our grandkids. Whether it's allowing them to stay up past bedtime or offering them a stack of warm cookies to munch on as they watch TV, we want their time with us to feel like a vacation. We enjoy pampering them, and they enjoy being pampered.

There's nothing wrong with a bit of indulgence now and then. But if we genuinely care about someone, we want their best. That includes doing what we can to keep them healthy as well as happy. An occasional slumber party is fun. A cookie or two for a snack isn't a crime. But too much sugar, too little sleep, and too many hours of screen time doesn't help our grandkids. It hurts them. That isn't our intention, but it's reality.

Let's be more intentional about helping our grandkids make healthier choices—and doing the same ourselves. The healthier we are, the better chance we having of sharing more time on this earth with those we love. Not only that: it's one way we can honor God.

Our bodies (and God's gift of life that we carry around in them) are priceless and irreplaceable. If we were given a priceless jewel, we wouldn't use it as a paperweight or toss it on the floor of our closet and forget about it. We'd treasure it, care for it, and wear it with pride. The same should be true of our precious bodies. Every time we make a healthy choice, it's like sending a thank-you note to God. The more we help these jewels shine, the more they can reflect their Creator's glory.

Dear Lord, I don't want to take this precious body you've given me (or my grandkids) for granted. If there's a bad habit I need to break, make me aware of it—and give me the strength and courage I need to change. Amen.

LOVE IN ACTION

Take a close look at the snacks you usually serve your grandkids. Is there anything you can do to make them healthier—while still making your grandkids feel treated?

35

Rooted in Faith

Before the world was made, God decided
to make us his own children through Jesus Christ.
That was what he wanted and what pleased him.

—EPHESIANS 1:5 ICB

With the current popularity of genealogical websites, surveying the roots and branches of our family tree has never been easier. Or more fun! Its gives us a sense of purpose and place, an assurance that we're one integral piece that's part of a bigger puzzle. We hold our head a little higher upon discovering we're related to some famous historical figure or have distant relatives who heralded from a country far across the sea. As for scoundrels we uncover along the way, we console ourselves with the knowledge that the past doesn't dictate the future. Just look how far we've come!

It's fun to pass along more than just unfamiliar names and faded family photos to our grandkids. We can enjoy telling them true stories about real people who share their heritage. Yet their heritage (and ours) isn't only a physical one. We share a spiritual heritage, as well. The Bible calls us heirs, brothers and sisters, descendants of Abraham, sons of the living God, and members of the household of faith. We come from a long line of sinners and saints whose stories we can read about in the pages of God's Word, as well as in biographies of spiritual trailblazers—such as William Wilberforce, Corrie ten Boom, Martin Luther, or Lottie Moon.

By acquainting our grandchildren with the depth and breadth of their physical and spiritual family tree, we can give them a deeper feeling of belonging, a clearer sense of identity, and a broader base of love. We can help them understand that being part of a "family" is truly something worth celebrating.

Dear Lord, thank you for making me part of this family—and yours. Please use me to help my grandkids better understand how they are an important part of a much bigger picture. Amen.

LOVE IN ACTION

Make a family tree for each of your grandkids. Link family members and ancestors together as the branches, then add your grandkids' favorite Bible characters as the spiritual roots that support the tree.

36

Expanding the "Grand" in Grandma

Religion that God the Father accepts is this:
caring for orphans or widows who need help.

—JAMES 1:27 ICB

Orphans don't have to be children without parents. They can be any child who feels abandoned, forgotten, and alone in a great big world. Perhaps they face the challenge of divorce, military deployment, a medical crisis, relocation, homelessness, or a death in the family. Maybe they come home from school to an empty house because their parents are working hard to pay the bills.

Unfortunately, not every child is lucky enough to have a grandmother like you to walk beside them during times like these. But God provides each one of us with an eternal supply of love. We can't use it up or wear it out. It grows bigger and stronger the more we exercise it. That means there's enough "grandma" in us to go around, regardless of how many grandchildren God blesses us with—including those we adopt along the way.

There are plenty of children within our own neighborhood, church, or our grandchildren's circle of friends who could use a little extra love in their lives. If we enlist the help of our grandchildren in making others feel like a part of the family, they are less likely to feel jealous and more likely to feel like an integral part of the rescue operation. If we happen to be widowed, reaching out beyond our family circle is even more important. Caring for others is one way God helps us better care for ourselves.

But first, we need eyes to see the need and a heart that's willing to risk reaching out. Let's invite God to expand the "grand" in us, becoming even grander grandmas as time goes by.

Dear Lord, show me any children you want me to lavish a little extra love on. Then, guide me in the best way to share that love—generously, tenderly, and faithfully. Amen.

LOVE IN ACTION

Talk to your grandchildren about children they personally know who could use a little extra grandmotherly love. Work together to come up with a plan for how to extend your love in a practical way. Then, do it!

37

No Matter What

May your roots go down deep into the soil of God's
marvelous love; and may you be able to feel and
understand, as all God's children should, how long,
how wide, how deep, and how high his love really is;
and to experience this love for yourselves.

—Ephesians 3:17–19 TLB

There's a depth and ferocity to a grandmother's love
that we can't quite explain or even fully understand.
Our general demeanor may be quiet and reserved, but
if our grandkids were ever in trouble, Grandmama Bear
would undoubtedly make an appearance. We'd protect
them with all that was in us, baring our claws if necessary.
We're their champion and cheerleader, ready to console,
encourage, forgive, celebrate, advocate, or do whatever

we believe is necessary to help them along in this world. We love them no matter what—and we can't imagine it any other way.

We didn't just fall in love with our grandchildren as we got to know them better. We loved them deeply even before they were born. They belonged to us and we belonged to them. That was enough for our beautiful bond to take root. But even the strongest love is still an imperfect love. Unless, of course, we're God himself.

God's love for our grandkids can't help but be perfect. He *is* love itself (1 John 4:8). If we read 1 Corinthians 13:4–8 and replace the word *love* with *God*, we're told that God "is kind and patient, never jealous, boastful, proud, or rude. [God] isn't selfish or quick tempered. [God] doesn't keep a record of wrongs that others do. [God] rejoices in the truth, but not in evil. [God] is always supportive, loyal, hopeful, and trusting. [God] never fails!" (CEV).

How good it is to know that God loves our grandchildren in the way that we wish we were capable of loving them. And how good it is to know he loves us that very same way.

Dear Lord, help me trust and rest in your love for me and my family. Show me how my love for others can grow to become more like yours. Amen.

LOVE IN ACTION

Memorize the thirteenth chapter of 1 Corinthians. Each morning, repeat it aloud as a prayer to God. Praise him for the faithfulness of his love and ask him to reveal to you how to better follow in his loving footsteps.

38

On the Road Again

We know that God causes everything to work
together for the good of those who love God and are
called according to his purpose for them.

—Romans 8:28 nlt

Have you ever wondered why being a grandmother seems to be more fun than being a parent? We joke about being able to hand our grandkids back to their parents when they're fussy, need their diaper changed, or when we simply need some "me time." But it's more than that. Part of our joy comes from having a broader perspective, one that includes decades of hindsight.

Let's face it: We've experienced parenting firsthand—and survived. We've also gone through hard times and have come out the other side. When we look back, we can see how God has taken the good and the bad and woven them together. He's used them to refine us, to help us mature, and to direct us toward where we are today. Our past provides perspective, teaching us not to "sweat the small stuff" (to use a modern cliché). It's also taught us that sometimes the small stuff is the most important.

As savvy travelers on the road of life, we have the opportunity to help the newbies navigate some of the twists and turns ahead. But, that means we must take the time to examine where we've been. We need to honestly admit when our own inattention or poor choices pointed us straight into a pothole. We also need to evaluate our lives so far, so we can gain a clearer perspective about how God has used the past in a positive way.

As we encourage our kids and grandkids as they travel so many unfamiliar roads at this season in their lives, we'll find we're strengthening our own faith at the same time. The more aware we are of how far we've come, the more gratitude we'll feel for God's guidance along the way.

Dear Lord, thank you for bringing purpose, and something positive, out of everything that happens in my life. When tough times come, help me remember what you've done so I will more readily lean on you. Amen.

LOVE IN ACTION

Keep a journal that specifically lists hard things you've been through—and the good things God has brought out of each of them. Consider it a spiritual heirloom you can pass on to your grandchildren one day.

39

Childproofing Gets Personal

A wise woman strengthens her family.
But a foolish woman destroys hers by what she does.

—Proverbs 14:1 ICB

When our grandkids are small, we childproof our house before they visit. We put breakables on a higher shelf, lock cabinets that contain cleaning products, cover electrical outlets, and put gates across stairways. Once they arrive, we lock the front door so inquisitive youngsters won't accidentally end up wandering down the street by themselves. We take precautions to keep them safe.

But our grandchildren are doing more than trying to check out the cabinet under the kitchen sink. They're also checking *us* out. As babies and toddlers, they're watching our facial expressions and listening to how we speak. As they get older, they're picking up clues about table manners, social mores, and how relationships work—including a relationship with God. Our grandkids learn more by observing the way we live than by anything we try to teach.

That means we need to childproof our lives. Is there anything we do or say that might be harmful for our grandkids to imitate? Negative attitudes? Mean-spirited sarcasm? Selfishness? Addictions to shopping, eating, or alcohol?

Personal "childproofing" begins by recognizing we have a problem. This takes honesty with ourselves and, sometimes, from a good friend who wants God's best in our lives. Next, we need to take a step toward positive change by asking God's forgiveness. Then, it's time to come up with a plan. What can we do to break a habit that we may have had for years? Asking a close friend to be an accountability partner for us in this area can help us stick with our goal for change.

Who knows? Our love for our grandkids may be just the motivation we need to push us in the direction God longs for us to go.

Dear Lord, I want to strengthen my family by being a positive influence on the lives of my grandkids. Please reveal to me any areas where I may be blind to my own failings, and give me the strength and wisdom to change. Amen.

LOVE IN ACTION

Do an assessment of your home *and* your heart, looking for anything that might prove harmful to your grandkids. If God reveals any changes that need to be made, don't ignore them. Write your goal on an index card and post it, along with a picture of your grandchildren, somewhere you'll see it every day.

40

Through a Grandmother's Eyes

Yes, all have sinned;
all fall short of God's glorious ideal.

—Romans 3:23 TLB

Our vision may not be quite as stellar as it was when we were young, but when a grandmother looks at her grandkids, she sees perfection. That's fine, as long as we know in our hearts that our grandkids are human. They're flawed and fallible, just like us.

If we don't keep this in mind, we may allow our love to blind us to the truth. We may refuse to accept that our grandkids would do anything dishonest, such as lie to us, steal money from our purse, or struggle with a drug or alcohol problem. Yes, we want to give our grandkids the benefit of the doubt, but that doesn't mean turning a blind eye, excusing bad behavior, and letting things slide—all in the name of love.

If this is the misguided way we "love" our grandkids, we may expect God to love us the very same way. After all, if God accepts us just the way we are, then why bother facing our faults, right? Yes, it's true that through Christ's sacrifice on the cross we're forgiven, once and for all. Nothing we do can keep us from spending eternity with him. But our choices may keep us from becoming the people God created us to be. That means heartbreak for both our Creator and for us.

We want our grandchildren to be the people we see with our "grandmother's eyes." This doesn't mean we "ideal-eyes" them. It means we see them for who they really are at this moment, while still being able to visualize the person we pray they'll become down the road. We hope for them to become the very best version of themselves—the individual God designed them to be.

Dear Lord, help me see my grandchildren through your eyes—wholly loved, but human. Show me how to love them well, especially when they turn away from who you created them to be. Amen.

LOVE IN ACTION

Keep the lines of communication open with your grown children. Ask them regularly if there are any specific areas they'd like you to pray about for your grandkids. Strive for honesty in all areas, steering clear of judgment or being too free with your advice, so they don't feel pressured to sugarcoat the truth.

41

The Best of Intentions

A person who promises a gift but doesn't give it
is like clouds and wind that bring no rain.

—Proverbs 25:14 NLT

When the unexpected happens—a flat tire, a freak snowstorm, a bout of the stomach flu, a bill you didn't know you'd have to pay—how do you respond? You promised you'd be there, do this, or pay for that. But then you can't, and it breaks your heart that you have to break your word. Or does it?

It's true, there will be times when we simply can't fulfill what we've promised our grandkids, no matter how hard we try. James 4:15 advises us to keep in mind that "our tomorrows are in the Lord's hands and if he is willing we will live life to its fullest and do this or that" (TPT).

Some days simply don't go as we'd planned. As a result, our grandkids wind up disappointed. When that happens, we need to apologize, remind our grandkids how much we love them, and then let ourselves off the hook. After all, God is the only one who's capable of being faithful to every promise he's ever made.

However, not all broken promises happen accidentally. Some are simply taken too lightly from the start. Sometimes we allow our musings to sound more like actual plans. Our "what if" or "maybe someday" can transform into "this is going to happen" in our grandkids' minds. Then anticipation kicks in, making our words reside even more deeply in their hopeful little hearts.

Yes, kids need to learn how to handle disappointment, but let's not be responsible for giving them a crash course. Let's be careful with our words, including our promises. Good intentions aren't good at all if we're wishy-washy on our follow-through.

Dear Lord, I want to be as good as my word. Help me follow through on my promises, even if they become inconvenient. Amen.

LOVE IN ACTION

Make a "Grandma Calendar" each month for your grandkids. Anytime you make a special plan or promise together, mark it on the calendar. Then, follow through. As they say in the business world, "If it isn't written, it isn't real."

42

Celebrating Sundays

This day belongs to the Lord!
Let's celebrate
and be glad today.
—Psalm 118:24 CEV

On their birthdays, we encourage our grandkids to make a wish and blow out their candles—even though we don't believe in the veracity of wishes. At Christmas, we stand in line with our grandkids so they can sit on Santa's lap and tell him everything they want—even though we know he can't deliver. On Thanksgiving, we gather together to eat a traditional meal of turkey, potatoes, and pumpkin pie—even though the first Thanksgiving didn't include potatoes or pie; it was more of a meat fest of venison, waterfowl, and possibly passenger pigeon.

We love celebrations and the rituals we associate with them—even if those rituals are nothing more than sentimental tradition. Is that what going to church has become for us? It's all too easy to go through the motions of worship by dressing up on Sunday, sitting in the same seat we always do, standing when we're supposed to stand, singing the words of songs we're barely listening to, and mentally planning where we're going for brunch as the pastor shares the morning message. If going to church is a meaningless ritual for us, we shouldn't be surprised if our grandchildren moan when we want them to join us.

Gathering together to worship God with our spiritual family, to listen to the love letters God has given us in his Word, and to remember Christ's sacrifice through the Lord's Supper is far from meaningless. But we have to help our grandkids understand why we do what we do. While we're at it, let's take time to remind ourselves.

Dear Lord, show me how to connect with you and my church family on a deeper level this Sunday. I don't want to simply show up; I want to celebrate who you are and all you've done. Amen.

LOVE IN ACTION

Are your grandchildren comfortable going to church with you when they visit? If you haven't checked out your church's children's ministry or youth group firsthand, it's time you did. Help your grandkids get excited about what they're going to see and do at church before Sunday morning rolls around.

43

Faithfully Focused

Marriage is honorable in every way, so husbands and
wives should be faithful to each other.

—HEBREWS 13:4 GW

At this stage in our lives, grandchildren can easily
become the focus of our love. If there's a grandpa in
the picture, that focus is skewed. We don't intend for it
to happen, but it's almost like we're having an affair. Our
thoughts, our time, our money, our energy, and our affection are headed in a new direction. And it isn't toward
the one we promised to love and cherish until death do
us part.

Besides taking our spouse for granted, we may also
view him as competition. Maybe the grandkids feel more
at home with him than they do with us. Or maybe he

feels that way about us. Regardless, neither jealousy nor complacency is God's design for marriage—even if our spouse is "unreasonable" or we've been married a very long time.

The Bible describes marriage as the most accurate illustration we have of our relationship with God. That relationship is intimate and exclusive, one that's supposed to grow deeper and richer over time, not slide into something old and tired. That takes effort on our part. We have to make sure our focus is directed toward loving well each and every day.

Even if death or divorce has severed our marriage relationship, it's still a part of our story—and our heart. The way we treat our spouse, our ex, or the memory of a spouse who went home to heaven before us will not go unnoticed by our grandkids. Our words and actions will tell them what marriage is like. Will the story we tell reflect God's own? It's up to us. Let's be faithful to our spouse in the little things as well as the big ones. Just the way we long to be in our relationship with God.

Dear Lord, thank you for my spouse and for the children and grandchildren you've brought into our lives because of our relationship. Teach me to love him like you do. Amen.

LOVE IN ACTION

Involve your grandkids in helping you plan an anniversary, birthday, or Father's Day surprise for Grandpa. Invite them to help you show your love for your spouse in creative, heartfelt ways.

44

Breathing Room

A believer should take care of his own relatives,
especially his own family. If he does not do that,
he has turned against the faith. He is worse than a
person who does not believe in God.

—1 TIMOTHY 5:8 ICB

As we age, we're gifted with grandmotherly bodies. For most women, that means we get a bit rounder and squishier as time goes by. What used to pass for a waist could now pass for a barrel. Such is life. But breaking in a new granny body requires that we make a few adjustments to our wardrobe. Good-bye bikini, hello drawstring pants. After all, few things are more uncomfortable than squeezing yourself into a pair of britches that are too tight.

The same thing could be said about family relations.

When we don't give one another room to breathe, things get uncomfortable. What makes things even more confusing is that what may feel comfortable to us may be too confining for our adult kids and grandkids. The only way to accurately gauge how much space our family needs is to communicate with one another, clearly, honestly, and consistently.

Even how much time we need to spend communicating is up for individual interpretation! How often we call or text, how frequently we drop by to visit, how long we stay, how close we decide to live to our grandkids, our expectations of "family time" on weekends and holidays … and the list goes on. What's comfortable for everyone in situations like these needs to be discussed, not assumed. To aid in an honest discussion, we need to say aloud that we won't allow our feelings to be hurt by the truth. And mean it.

Our sole intention may be to care for our family. That's not only commendable but God's will for us. Sometimes we care for them by giving them space. Even though we may long for more time with them, loving them well means putting what they need ahead of what we want.

Dear Lord, I want to be sensitive to the needs of my family, without playing the martyr. Show me when to draw close and when to give them room—and how to do it. Amen.

LOVE IN ACTION

Prayerfully set up a time to chat with your grown children to discuss how they're doing and what they need from you at this time. Talk about boundaries on both sides of the relationship. Check in regularly to make certain nothing has changed. Do so with honesty, integrity, and grace.

45

Enough Is Enough

Jesus continued, "Be alert and guard your heart
from greed and always wishing for what you don't
have. For your life can never be measured by
the amount of things you possess."

—LUKE 12:15 TPT

We've seen them on the news. They're older women,
just like us, but something's gone terribly wrong.
Their homes are filled to the brim with trash, collectables,
or cats. Maybe all three. We shake our heads, wondering,
How did they ever let it get that bad? But chances are, we
have more in common than we care to admit.

Anytime we use "stuff" to try and make ourselves
happy, we're hoarding. We're surrounding ourselves with
more than we need. What's worse, we encourage our

grandkids to slide into this very same rut. How? When we celebrate their accomplishments, show them we love them, and try to dry their tears all the very same way—by buying them a gift.

Greed isn't something reserved for Wall Street tycoons. It resides in well-meaning grandmothers too. We console ourselves by saying we have just an itty-bitty proclivity toward shopping. But the more we continue acquiring stuff for ourselves, or as gifts for others, the less content we really are.

We're discontented because we're filling our hearts with counterfeit goods. They may promise a lot of things, but they simply can't deliver. Our hearts were designed to be satisfied by only one thing: God himself.

Although we've invited God into our hearts, we may have only opened up a tiny closet for Him to live in. The rest may still be crammed full of stuff, just like a hoarder's home. One by one, we need to sift through what we're holding onto other than God: prestige, financial freedom, a designer home, the hope of a fairy-tale romance. Not everything will be tangible, but it's all expendable. The more room we allow for God in our heart, the more content—and less greedy—we'll become.

Dear Lord, help me know when to say "enough" in any area of my life where I'm tempted to overindulge. When I'm feeling discontent, show me how to fill my restless heart with more of you. Amen.

LOVE IN ACTION

Instead of always giving your grandchildren "stuff" for special occasions, give them experiences. Make a coupon booklet with vouchers for things like a trip to the zoo, a visit to an ice cream parlor, or a night together at the movies.

46

Every Tear Counts

You've kept track of all my wandering
and my weeping.
You've stored my many tears in your bottle—
not one will be lost.
You care about me every time I've cried. For it is all
recorded in your book of remembrance.

—Psalm 56:8 tpt

Loss, fear, betrayal, rejection, disappointment, pain ... there are plenty of situations that will cause us to weep in this life. Unfortunately, little hearts break just like big ones. And when our grandchildren are faced with heartache and pain, we'd do anything to make it stop. What will we do to try to comfort them? Probably whatever we do to try to comfort ourselves.

We all have our preferred coping mechanisms when it comes to seeking solace. We call a friend or seek out a hug. We pull up the covers and hide from the world. We drown our sorrows with a glass of wine or a big bowl of ice cream. We distract ourselves with a movie or binge-watch TV. We suck it up and keep going. Regardless of where we turn first when we're hurting, hopefully we also reach out to God somewhere along the way.

What would happen if we reached out to Him first? Perhaps we'd make better choices with what we do next. If we didn't run quite so quickly to self-medicate, God could lead us toward things that will help us heal, instead of just numbing the pain. Isn't that what we really want for our grandchildren? Both comfort and healing?

If our grandchild came to us in tears with a cut on her finger, we wouldn't give her a decongestant. We'd clean the wound and give her a bandage. True, swallowing a dose of medicine would be less painful than putting anti-septic on an open wound, but it wouldn't do anything but prolong her pain.

Let's treat the wounds of this world wisely, whether they're ours or our grandchildren's. When we're in pain, let's make reaching out to God our default setting.

Dear Lord, help me think clearly when my grandkids or I am in pain. Help us find comfort in your presence and your promise of healing. Amen.

LOVE IN ACTION

When your grandchildren are in pain, physically or emotionally, give them a tiny bottle to keep by their bedside. Tie a card containing the words of Psalm 56:8 to it. Tell them that anytime they feel like crying, they can hold the bottle to remind them to talk to God. If he counts each of their tears, he certainly cares about everything they're going through.

47

Leaning on the Everlasting Arms

[God said,] "My power shows up best in weak people."
Now I am glad to boast about how weak I am; I am glad
to be a living demonstration of Christ's power, instead
of showing off my own power and abilities.

—2 Corinthians 12:9 tlb

We all begin as weaklings in this world. We can't walk, talk, or dress ourselves. Without others to feed us, we wouldn't survive. As we grow older, we hopefully grow stronger and more independent; but that only happens when we risk doing things on our own. Taking our first step unassisted. Removing the training wheels from our bike. Getting our driver's license. The list grows as we mature.

Grandmothers can help, or hinder, this process. We refuse to let go of a toddler's hand because she might topple over. We tie our grandson's shoes for him because it's more expedient. We pay for our teenage granddaughter's mission trip, instead of letting her earn the money, because we want to help. When we develop a pattern of doing for our grandchildren what they should be learning to do for themselves, we've confused serving with enabling.

If we love our grandchildren—really—we want them to mature. That means helping them learn to become self-sufficient, while at the same time becoming Christ dependent. One does not cancel out the other. It's like walking on a tightrope. We have to keep leaning, adjusting, and correcting to keep moving forward. We lean on our own abilities, then lean into Christ when we need power that exceeds our own, which allows us to lean back and do what he's guiding us to do.

Christ is the only safety net our grandchildren have. Not us. It's fine for us to lend them a helping hand, as long as that hand is moving them forward, not holding them back.

Dear Lord, help me give my grandchildren enough room to grow and mature. Teach them, and me, how to trust and depend more on you. Amen.

LOVE IN ACTION

When the opportunity lends itself, talk to your grandchildren about the positive side of weakness. How does our dependence on God and others encourage us to build relationships? To stay humble? To trust God?

48

Fretter's Anonymous

Don't fret or worry. Instead of worrying, pray.
Let petitions and praises shape your worries into
prayers, letting God know your concerns.

—Philippians 4:6 msg

Grandmothers are often portrayed as worrywarts. They wring their hands, furrow their brows, and say things like, "I only worry because I love you!" But, as singer Tina Turner would say, "What's love got to do with it?" Worry and anxiety don't stem from love. They're rooted in a lack of control.

We worry our grandbaby will catch a cold—because his mother dressed him, not us. We worry about our granddaughter heading off to college—because we aren't there to lock the door at night and make certain she doesn't get in with the wrong crowd. The list goes on and on. Worrying over situations that are out of our control can tie us up in emotional knots. And it doesn't teach our grandchildren how much we love them. It models for them what it's like to live in fear.

That's where prayer comes in. When we take each of our worries and fashion it into a prayer, we take it straight to the only one who *is* in control—God. When we share our concerns with God, something wonderful happens. The next verse in Philippians that follows the one above tells us, "Before you know it, a sense of God's wholeness, everything coming together for good, will come and settle you down. It's wonderful what happens when Christ displaces worry at the center of your life" (Philippians 4:7 MSG).

If we truly love our grandchildren (and we know we do), then what we'll want at the center of their lives is Christ, displacing worry and fear. If that's our desire for them, let's begin by choosing that for ourselves.

Dear Lord, you know even better than I do what's weighing down my heart and tying my emotions in knots. One by one, I want to give my worries to you. Please show me how. Amen.

LOVE IN ACTION

Instead of letting anxious thoughts go around and around in your mind, write your worries on an index card. Hold that card as you pray to God about each of your concerns. Then, throw the card in the fireplace or trash as a physical reminder that these concerns are no longer yours. They're in God's hands now.

49

Memory Keeper

All day we parade God's praise—
we thank you by name over and over.

—Psalm 44:8 msg

When we purchase a picture frame, we don't put it on display with the advertising photo that came with it. Why have some random family we've never met smiling back at us from our mantel? We want to fill it with the faces of those we know and love. That includes our grandkids. That way, every time we see their image, we're flooded with loving memories of our time together. If we let them, those memories can lead us straight to praising God.

Instead of photos, the Israelites used rocks to do the same thing. They didn't have a cell phone to capture the moment when they finally crossed the Jordan River into the Promised Land, so they made a pile of stones. Then, every time they saw these stones, they'd remember that God did something amazing on this very spot—and they'd stop to say thank you.

God has done so many amazing things in our lives, including allowing us the blessing of becoming grand-mothers. But we get busy, distracted, disheartened over what's going on in the world, and we forget all of the rea-sons to be grateful. We forget to turn to God in thanks, instead of only when we're feeling sad, angry, or needy.

Praising God for his goodness isn't just a gift for him. It's a morale boost for us. When we stop to count our blessings, something happens—our heart gets lighter. Our good memories are like buoys God uses to help keep us afloat during troubled times. With our heads above water, it's easier for us to keep our eyes on God and see what wonderful things he has for us waiting on the horizon.

Dear Lord, thank you for your goodness. I'm blessed in so many wonderful ways and humbled by how rich I am in the things that matter most. Amen.

LOVE IN ACTION

Follow the Israelites' footsteps by creating some stones of remembrance in your own home. Make quilt squares, a photo collage, or a literal pile of stones to remind you of significant blessings God has brought into your life. Put it somewhere that will frequently remind you to thank God for all he's done.

50

Mirror, Mirror, on the Wall ...

"The LORD does not look at the things people
look at. People look at the outward appearance, but
the LORD looks at the heart."

—1 SAMUEL 16:7

"Cute!" Is there any word we hear more when our grandkids first come into the world? Whether it's for her smile, his chubby cheeks, the rolls on his thighs, or the outfit she's wearing, the majority of compliments babies receive center on their appearance. Of course, at this point in their lives, there's not much else we can comment on. Their compassion, quick wit, and athletic ability have yet to be revealed. But even as our grandkids mature and their personality, abilities, and strength of character become evident to all, their appearance is still the focus of more discussion and thought than is beneficial.

We're a body-conscious culture—and what's "in" graces the cover of a magazine. Yeah, those airbrushed, photo-shopped, flawless faux people. When too much emphasis is put on how we appear in the mirror, our attractiveness (as weighed against the magazine standard, either by others or ourselves) gets all muddled up with our worth. This can play havoc with the mind and the heart.

Are we doing anything to reinforce this misconception? Do we repeatedly put ourselves down, pointing out how overweight, old, or out of shape we are? Do we refuse to wear a swimsuit in public? Do we make negative comments about people we pass on the street? Do we voice our disapproval of our grandchildren's avant-garde clothing or hairstyles?

God provides the only mirror that really counts in this life. The more favorably we reflect his image, the more attractive we become. Literally. People are attracted to those who are loving, generous, patient, and kind. So let's silence our criticism and save our compliments for what really matters. Let's catch our grandchildren being beautiful on the inside. Then we can tell them how incredibly attractive they really are.

Dear Lord, help me focus more on reflecting you than on my reflection in the mirror. Thank you for the body you've given me, and please forgive me when I treat it with disregard or disrespect. Amen.

LOVE IN ACTION

Make two signs to post on the bathroom mirror: one for your grandkids and one for yourself. Write on them, "God sees me from the inside out. So, how do I look today?"

51

Stage Grandma

Our lives get in step with God and all others
by letting him set the pace, not by proudly
or anxiously trying to run the parade.

—Romans 3:28 MSG

Role-playing can be fun. Just ask our grandkids. They dress up like superheroes, science fiction personas, or characters from a graphic novel so they can live out their favorite fantasy at Comic-Con. They play video games so they can drive a fast car, fly off a ski jump, or battle a mythical creature. They enjoy walking in someone else's shoes for a while. Someone whose shoes they'd never have a chance to fill in real life.

We do the same thing, but sometimes the shoes we try to cram our proverbial feet into belong to our grandchildren. We get so wrapped up in their lives that at times we confuse theirs with our own. Their victories, and failures, begin to feel as though they belong to us. So do their plans for the future.

How can we tell? When we're heartbroken because they switch their dance class for karate (and we always wanted to take ballet, but our parents couldn't afford the lessons). When we push too hard for them to attend our alma mater for college. Whenever we feel disappointed because the choices our grandchildren make differ from those we'd make in the same situation.

God gives us only one life to live: our own. When we try to live vicariously through our grandchildren, we pressure them to become who we want them to be—or who we wish we could be. In the process, we lose sight of who God created them to be, which is guaranteed to be much more amazing than anything else we have in mind.

Let's let our grandkids go, and grow, to become who they are. There's only one pair of shoes in this world they can fill. And our feet won't fit in there with them.

Dear Lord, help me accept that my own life is enough. Show me how to make the most of each and every day you bring my way. Amen.

LOVE IN ACTION

Use shoe shopping as a time to talk to your grandkids about God's unique plan for their lives. As they try on different shoes, discuss how it takes a while to find the ones that are comfortable, appropriate, and fit just right. Explain how growing up feels kind of the same way. We try on different occupations, relationships, and even churches before we find where we fit comfortably in the world.

52

Hello, Good-Bye ...

Every time I think of you in my prayers, which is
practically all the time, I ask [God] to clear the way
for me to come and see you. The longer this waiting
goes on, the deeper the ache. I so want to be there
to deliver God's gift in person and watch you grow
stronger right before my eyes! But don't think I'm
not expecting to get something out of this, too! You
have as much to give me as I do to you.

—ROMANS 1:10–12 MSG

Life is a series of beginnings and endings, hellos and
good-byes. We say hello to this great, big world only by
saying good-bye to the comfort and safety of the womb.
We greet the opportunities and responsibilities of adulthood when we bid adieu to living under our parents' roof.

We can only welcome grandchildren into our lives after we've left our own youth behind. It's all a trade-off, each passing season linked by a bridge that leads from one blessing to the next.

Every visit with our grandchildren holds its own hello and good-bye, whether we see these precious faces every day or once in a blue moon. When it's time to go, it's tempting to rush through our farewells, focusing on the promise of "see you soon." But, we never know what tomorrow holds.

The older we get, the more acutely aware we become that there's a final good-bye somewhere in our future, one that heralds our first hello to heaven. What makes the thought of this wonderful day bittersweet is those we leave behind. Yes, we hold tightly to the hope that we'll be together again in God's presence one day, but no one really knows what that will be like. So we move forward in faith, as we revel in the gift of today.

There's a Native American proverb that says, "When you were born, you cried and the world rejoiced. Live your life so that when you die, the world cries and you rejoice." Let's be grandmothers worth missing, women who've left their mark of God's love on the world and made a positive, eternal difference in their grandchildren's lives.

Dear Lord, I cannot thank you enough for your gift of my grandchildren. Help me relish every moment I spend with them and be a constant blessing in their lives. Amen.

LOVE IN ACTION

Write love letters for your grandchildren to open at their graduation, on their wedding day, at the birth of their first child, and even when they become grandparents themselves. Put them in the children's baby books for safekeeping until the day arrives for them to be opened.